Dog Training Basics

All-In-One Startup Guide: 5 Standard Commands, 4 Essential Training Concepts & House Training For Beginners

By Vivaco Books

Table of Contents

Introduction

What This Book Is About

This book contains proven methods and solid information regarding dog training from a beginner's perspective. It was designed with simplicity in mind and as a short guide that will provide you with all the necessary information regarding dog training so as to make better choices.

You are most likely a new dog owner, or maybe you owned a dog before, but never tried to train it properly. In any case, adding a dog into you and your family's life is a big commitment. Training a dog takes time, effort and patience. It may seem difficult at times, but the reward of having a healthy trained furry friend is definitely worth it.

You are going to learn what dog training is and why it is so important. We have summarized the most popular training methods available, so you can find out which one would best suit you and your canine.

You will learn the 4 most important basic training concepts, which you can apply instantly and see results, regardless of training methods.

You will also find out the 5 standard commands that every dog owner should know and every dog should follow, in order to have a healthy and happy relationship with each other.

Finally, if you intend to keep your dog inside your home, you will learn some house manners that your dog should understand and follow, so that it won't bring down your house.

Thank you for purchasing this book. We hope you enjoy it!

Chapter 1:

What Everyone Ought To Know About Dog Training

Dog training refers to the modification process of a dog behavior, either for the dog to help in particular activities or perform specific tasks, or for the dog to effectively participate in typical domestic life.

While dog training for particular duties goes way back, their training to be compatible pets started in the 1950s. The dog learns from each interaction that it has with the environment. This chapter highlights what dog training focuses on to achieve the training purpose.

How Dogs Learn

Operant/Instrumental conditioning

This form of learning allows a dog's behavior to be modified by the consequences. There are 2 complementary motivations that drive instrumental learning: the minimization of aversive outcomes and the maximization of positive ones.

There are basically two methods of reinforcing or strengthening behavior: Positive Reinforcement is where a behavior becomes strengthened by the production of certain desirable consequences while Negative Reinforcement is where a behavior becomes strengthened by the avoidance of some undesirable consequences.

Typical positive reinforcement situations satisfy certain psychological and physiological needs; hence it can be in the form of food, demonstration of affection or a game. Different dogs find various things reinforcing. Negative reinforcement happens when the dog discovers that a specific response terminates the presentation of any aversive stimulus. Aversive may be anything that a dog doesn't like; for example, a tight choking chain.

Classical conditioning

This is a form of learning where a single stimulus, the conditioned one, signals a second stimulus to occur, the unconditioned stimulus.

Classical conditioning is basically when the dog learns to familiarize itself with things in the environment, or realizes that certain things go together. The dog may be frightened of rain by associating it with lightning and thunder, or the dog may respond to its owner putting on a specific pair of shoes by getting its leash.

This method is employed in dog training to aid it in making particular associations with a specific stimulus, in order to overcome fear of situations or people.

Non-associative learning

This is a response change to stimulus that does not include association of the presented stimulus with an event or even another stimulus like punishment or reward. There are two forms of non-associative learning: habituation and sensitization.

A good example of habituation is when a dog that often reacts excitedly to a door alarm is subjected to repeated ringing until it stops responding to this meaningless stimuli.

The dog will become habituated to such a noise. Some reactions to stimuli may become stronger rather than habituating to repeated event or stimuli. This is where desensitization comes in handy.

Desensitization involves pairing positive reactions with objects, people, or conditions that causes anxiety or fear. Consistent exposure to feared objects or rewards, such as fireworks, reduces the dog's stress, thereby making it desensitized.

Social learning

This is influenced by the behavior of others. It does not require reinforcement to take place, but rather a model. It involves observing, remembering and imitating behaviors.

Domestic dogs are social animals and their social dependency enables them to learn the behavior of other dogs.

The term "social learning" covers many closely linked concepts: mimicking or allelomimetic behavior where puppies copy others, social facilitation where another dog causes increased behavior intensity and local enhancement that includes social facilitation pieces, trial-and-error learning and mimicking.

Chapter 2:

How To Choose The Right

Training Method

Dog training involves teaching a dog to obey various commands given by the master. There are various dog training methods and each of them has its own share of advantages and disadvantages. People who are looking for the right dog training method for their pet must consider the amount of time they would devote to dog training, their patience, how smart their dog appears to be, as well as the dog's preferences.

The characteristics of any successful method include knowing your dog's personality and attributes, accuracy in timing reinforcement or punishment, as well as consistent communication. Here are the major dog training methods you can choose depending on the above factors.

Dog Training Methods

Koehler Method

The Koehler method is based on the philosophy that dogs often act on their rights to choose their actions. The method emphasizes that every dog's learned behavior/action is a matter of choice which solely depends on their personal learning experience. When these choices are driven by the expectation of some reward, such a behavior will probably be repeated.

On the other hand, when they are driven by anticipation of some sort of punishment, they will likely go away. Once your dog learns that the choices lead to discomfort or comfort, it can then be taught to always make the right decisions.

Action-Memory-Desire is the learning pattern that this method employs; the dog will act, remember the consequences, and then form the willingness to avoid or repeat the consequences.

Adherents of this method often believe that after a behavior has been taught correctly, it should be enacted so that any subsequent correction would be fair, expected and reasonable.

This method has been used for several years, but some of the prescribed punishment procedures are now considered unnecessary, inappropriate and inhumane by several trainers.

Motivational Training

Motivational or positive training uses reward in reinforcing good behavior, while ignoring the bad behavior.

This is based on Thorndike's Law of Effect which states that actions that result in rewards will become more frequent and those that don't result in rewards will become less frequent.

Pure positive dog training is possible, but hard, as it calls for patience and time to regulate the rewards that the dog gets for its behavior.

Clicker training

This is a positive reinforcement dog training system that depends on operant conditioning. It employs conditioned reinforcers that are delivered more rapidly and precisely as compared to primary reinforcers like food.

The key to effective delivery of this dog training method is accurate timing by delivering a particular conditioned reinforcer at the time when a desired behavior is exhibited. The clicker focuses on entrenching a good behavior in a dog by luring it by using reinforcers such as hand gestures or treats. After the dog learns the behavior, the treat and the clicker is stopped.

Clicker training does not employ physical corrections or compulsions. It is majorly based on positive reinforcements.

Certain clicker trainers employ mild corrections like a non-reward marker: "Whoops" or "Uhuh" to make the dog realize that a behavior is not right, or corrections like "Time out" in which attention to the dog is withdrawn.

Electronic training

This entails the use of an aversive tool like an electric shock. Common types include remotely triggered collars or those that can be triggered by barking, fencing which gives a shock when a dog with a special collar goes over a buried wire, and special mats placed on the furniture to give some type of shock. Certain aids produce an aversive like citronella spray when triggered.

Electronic dog training has generated a lot of controversy. Those who support it say that employing electronic device in training dogs permits distance training and can eliminate self-rewarding behavior.

They also claim that if well used, they have a reduced risk of injury and stress compared to mechanical devices, like choke chains.

Opponents point out the serious risks of psychological and physical trauma that can be caused by abusive or incorrect use.

Model-rival training

Based on social learning principles, this type of training employs a model and a rival for attention in demonstrating the desired behavior. This training method was initially used by Irene Pepperberg in training a parrot to label various objects.

After that, Young and McKinley undertook a study whether this method can be used to train domestic dogs.

The study generated the required results since the origin and nature of the dog allows observational learning.

Dominance-based training

This is based on the belief that "dogs are wolves" and because wolves have hierarchical packs in which the alpha male rules, humans must therefore dominate dogs so as to modify their behavior.

Animal behaviorists claim that the use of dominance in modifying the behavior may suppress the dog's behavior without solving the root cause of a problem. It may exacerbate a problem and elevate the dog's aggression, fear, and anxiety.

Dogs subjected to continuous threats might react aggressively. This may happen because the dogs feel afraid and threatened and not because they are trying to acquire dominance.

Relationship-based training

This is derived from symbolic interactionism theories and uses the patterns of adjustment, communication, and interpretation between the trainers and the dogs.

By building a positive relationship, this method intends to achieve results which will benefit the trainer and the dog alike as well as strengthen and enhance their relationship.

The fundamental principles include:

Making sure the dog's basic needs are met prior to commencing training.

Knowing what motivates the canine and employing that to influence its behaviors.

\# Interpreting the dog's body language for better communication between you and the dog.

\# Using positive reinforcement for desired behavior.

\# Teaching compatible behaviors instead of unwanted behaviors.

\# Controlling its environment to prevent unwanted behaviors.

In conclusion someone should take into consideration many factors prior to choosing the right training method that will be best suited for him as well as his dog.

Chapter 3:
The 4 Most Important Dog Training Concepts

When you bring a dog home, it needs more than just care, love and other basic needs. For a healthy and good dog/ human relationship, dog training is necessary as this enables it to learn the mannerisms needed to survive in society.

Each discipline stems around specific basic

principles. Animal behavior and dog training is no different. There are some basic dog training concepts that guide the whole process.

Basic Dog Training Concepts

Manage

Management hinders undesired behaviors from developing into habits by reducing or eliminating opportunities for dogs to rehearse such a behavior and hence develop an environment where a dog is always "correct" by default. It includes things like puppy proofing, leash use, crate training, using no-pull device, etc. It can be used together with rewards for success.

For instance, one can use no-pull devices for the dog to walk well on the leash, and reward him if he manages to walk at your side. Once the dog learns the behavior, fade out the tool and rewards gradually.

Reward

The reward can include anything the dog desires and will work for to earn. The common type is food, but toys, petting, play, and praise are better rewards for some dogs. It can also be an opportunity to do something it enjoys, like going through open doors, playing with other dogs, chasing after a rabbit, or being permitted to sit on the couch.

These real life rewards are often underutilized yet they are very powerful. Integrating these rewards in your routine interactions with the dog, will give you the opportunity to train it frequently without additional effort or extra gear.

Giving the dog rewards without earning them will eventually make the rewards meaningless. A dog wouldn't want to work if it is able to get privileges and rewards for free. Most people grasp this quickly since it applies to meals, but the same logic applies to other rewards.

Allowing the dog to run through the door at will is not safe and also eliminates potentially better opportunities to reward him for good behavior. The dog should sit and watch you as you open the door. Release the dog only after complying with the command.

Ignore

Simply ignore any irritating behavior and the dog will stop it with time. Be selective on the behaviors to ignore. Some of them are self-reinforced and tend to worsen if ignored, like chewing on all items, marking inside the house, or cat chasing. The technique is more effective when your dog is trying to get attention, like jumping on people, begging for a meal, hand nudging, barking for a treat or attention. When demanding attention, even negative attention like scolding can be seen as a reward.

These bad attention-seeking behaviors will diminish faster if you ignore them, although they can become worse temporarily before the dog gives up. Be consistent and ensure the dog ignores any unwanted behavior all the time, or it won't work.

Correct

Offering rewards or ignoring bad behavior won't work if there is something more rewarding in its environment. Harassing wild animals, cats, or livestock, jumping on kids or grabbing clothes or car chasing are examples of self-reinforcing and enjoyable behaviors in dogs that can be very dangerous too. In such cases, correcting or punishing the dog's behavior is appropriate.

Correcting a dog for undesired behavior is a popular concept. It's however important to know that "correcting" doesn't necessarily mean "punishing," it means fixing or making it right.

For instance, one can correct the dog's position by making it stand or sit gently, or tugging the drag line. This isn't really punishing, the dog has simply been shown to do the "correct" thing.

One should consider punishment only after they have performed preliminary work with the use of other methods, beginning with low destruction level up to highly demanding situations. One shouldn't punish their dogs for anything that they haven't taught them adequately.

Manage the highly distracting conditions while you train your dog up through gradually increasing distractions. When a given correction is necessary, one should employ the minimal punishment or correction to get the work done. This will mainly rely on your dog's temperament, training level, and also the distraction level.

When correcting your dog, focus on helping him to make the "right" decisions next time, rather than taking out your frustrations on him or showing him who the boss is.

Chapter 4:

The 5 Standard Commands Every Dog Should Know

Dogs can be great companions, but to enjoy their company more, there are some dog obedience rules that owners must teach their pet dogs. One obvious benefit of teaching your dog obedience is discipline.

When the dog responds to commands such as "stay,"

"sit," or "come," their management in public or at home, especially with larger breeds, becomes a blessing. Here are the basic obedience commands for every dog.

Basic Obedience Commands For Dogs

Sit

The aim of this command is to make the dog sit on his hindquarters while the front part of the body is placed on the front legs. It can be taught in three different ways.

The first one requires you to watch when the dog is about to sit and if he tries to do so, give the command "sit" in a clear and loud manner. Praise him once the hindquarters reach the ground.

Puppies react to this training technique quite fast. But older dogs may need a dog training treat. Stand in front of your dog and then guide the treat from the dog's nose towards the head. Keep it some centimeters over the head. As he trails the smell of the treat, his rear will drop to the ground while the front part will remain on the front legs.

The next technique is training the dog using a leash. Here, stand next to the dog while facing the same direction as the dog. Hold the leash straight and while saying "sit", push the dog's rump down, letting him sit down on the hind legs.

Down

You can start teaching this command by first getting the dog to sit down. Stand facing the dog while holding the dog treat on its nose and take it lower. Once the dog's belly is down and the front legs stretched out, give it the treat and then praise him.

If the dog fails to stretch out the front legs, move the treat horizontally and slowly away.

After the pet understands the non-verbal command, use the verbal command. Next time say the command as you lower the treat. The dog will be able to link the action with the command sooner.

Stay

Understanding the "down" and "sit" commands only don't show the dog's ability to understand commands. If the dog simply obeys a command and leaves once it's executed, you will lose the aim of teaching the commands.

Therefore, the dog should be taught to uphold the two initial commands till the release instruction is given. You can achieve this by training the dog to respect the "stay" command. Only teach this command once the dog has understood the previous two.

Stand facing the dog and then instruct it to either "down" or "sit." Keep eye contact and stay this way for one or two seconds. Praise the dog and offer him some treat and this will indicate the end of training time.

As he gets comfortable with shorter intervals of time, extend the time of upholding the "stay" position. After he reliably responds to this training level, add the verbal cue to your command.

Stand facing the dog and once he complies with the "down" or "sit" command, say "stay" while stretching out your hand with the palm facing him.

Come

This is the easiest command to teach, particularly for puppies. A puppy often sticks to the owner and enjoys playing around their feet. Getting him to his master isn't hard. Trying to get away from him may prove difficult.

Start with shorter distances. Step a couple of feet away from the puppy/dog. Hold a treat, kneel down and then call out the pet's name and command. For instance, "Tracy, come." With open arms, invite the dog to come.

As the dog starts to move in your direction, praise him. If he goes astray, quit praising and say the command again. If the dog starts walking towards you again, praise him. Reward the dog with praise and a treat once he reaches where you are.

Leave it

Teaching the dog the "leave it" command is valuable for several reasons. It keeps the dog safe. In case you drop medicine accidentally on the floor, he will leave it if told to. If there are broken glasses, simply utter "leave it." Use the command on anything you don't want the dog to interfere with.

The easiest way in teaching the "leave it" command is by using something that the dog wants, such as a toy or a treat. Choose something small that you can hold inside your palm.

While holding the treat with your fingers make sure that

you let the dog to see, smell and even lick it. Then say the "leave it" command and move your hand away from him.

If he tries to follow your hand simply close your palm without letting him get to the treat. Only when he calms down or loses interest show him the treat, say the "leave it" command and again move your hand away. If he tries to grab it just close your palm with the treat inside.

Chapter 5:

House Manners For Dogs

When one has a dog in the house, particularly around the kids, they will want the dog to have some good house manners. This simply means that the dog is not hyperactive and will stay calm.

A dog with good house manners should not bother the kids while they are eating, or grab food off the table or counter. A dog that has house manners doesn't get into the garbage, eliminate on the floor or lay on the couch.

Rather, a good dog should be well behaved and be able to follow commands and rules. Here are some common house manners that dogs are expected to uphold as well as tips on how to teach them each manner.

House Essentials For Dogs

Staying within the designated area

Designate a place for the dog to stay in. This can be a crate, a dog bed, or a mat. Take your dog to the designated place and motivate him to stay right there. Give the dog treats and praise him.

Giving the dog a chew toy will aid in keeping it contented. It is advisable to get a crate for the dog since it will see it as a sanctuary. This will serve as a place to leave your dog in case you are going out of the house for some time.

Obeying the "leave it" command

After being quiet for about 10 minutes in the designated place, take him on a leash around the house. Point objects you may want him to just leave alone, and say "no" or "leave it."

The dog will obviously not understand this immediately and so you must redo this exercise repeatedly. If the dog insists on chewing things in your house, spray the objects with a bitter apple spray every 24 hours.

This is more effective when coupled with the "leave it" or "no" command.

Eliminating outside and not on the floor

Teach the dog to potty outside. When the dog is still learning manners, leash or put it in his crate. Be keen on the signals so that you take him outside before he actually relieves himself on the floor. While walking him around, praise him when he does well. They will figure out this very quickly and the secret is to be consistent.

Not bothering people when eating

Teach the dog not to beg, whine or jump up to get food from the table. You can achieve this by teaching him the "stay/down" command. Hold a treat, bring it close to the ground and then utter, "Down." In case he just bends the head to the treat, don't offer him the treat. Once he is down, give him the treat.

Teach him the "stay" command by gesturing stop with your hand as you say "stay." Slowly back away. If the dog attempts to follow, utter "no" and then walk him to his original position. Keep him in stay/down position a bit far from the table as you eat.

Not jumping on people

Teach the dog never to jump on strangers or you. When the dog jumps on you, utter "off", face away and ignore him completely until he is down. Once he's down, praise him well and show affection. The same should apply when the dog jumps on another person.

In conclusion, dogs are great pets. They are loyal and loving. With proper training, they will behave well in the house. Teach them like you will teach your kids, with patience and love.

Chapter 6:

F.A.Q. - Frequently Asked Questions

What is dog training?

The term dog training has several meanings. First, we have "behavior dog training" in which the dog is trained to be a "good citizen." This typically includes house training, reasonable leash manners, good behavior while they are around other dogs and people and other related things which make him a better companion.

We also have "obedience training," which generally teaches the dog how to do specific activities.

Finally, there is "activity training" which focuses on particular activities – like hunting, herding, lure coursing, search and rescue and other related activities that are used to showcase the capabilities of the dog.

How can I choose the right training?

There is no wrong or right training. There are training techniques that are more effective compared to others under some circumstances.

The things that one needs to take into consideration when they are choosing an effective method for their dogs include: their personality, the dog's personality, their goals and abilities as a trainer, and their experience as a trainer.

What is the difference between corrections and rewards?

Reward leads to an increase in a particular behavior while correction leads to the reduction in a particular behavior.

Rewards should be given such that they increase the behavior in question, meaning that it has to be something that motivates the dog and he enjoys too.

Why should I train my dog?

There are many numerous valid reasons why you should train a dog. It helps build the relationship between you and the dog, allows you to condition him to behave as you desire, and it enables you and the canine to live harmoniously.

Training is important in preventing undesired behaviors. Well trained dogs are often welcomed and liked in the entire society and neighborhood. Families who have well trained dogs are much happier because their dogs are always very eager to do some work for them.

According to experts, dog training is also healthy for dogs. In fact, many bad behavioral problems develop from lack of exercise.

Is it true that some dog breeds are "un-trainable?"

There is a perception that some dog breeds, such as the Beagles, are "un-trainable." But this is not the case, as all kinds of breeds from wolf hybrids to terriers to hounds can be trained well.

When is the right time to begin dog training?

Raising a pup is just like raising a baby. You should start training your puppy at an early stage, but it shouldn't be too early.

The right time to start training the puppy is from six to eight weeks. The puppy should learn habit-forming things at an early stage.

Which behavioral problems can dog training programs solve?

There are many behavioral problems that training can address. The common ones include jumping on people, destructive chewing, play biting, nuisance barking, getting on the furniture, and housebreaking.

Who is the boss when training the dog?

You must put some limits and rules so that the pet knows how it's required to behave. However, you don't have to instill good behaviors by force like pinning the pet on his side or pulling the choke chain.

Train your pets by rewarding their good behaviors as

soon as they successfully accomplish them and ensure that they are not rewarded for bad behavior.

Does positive reinforcement training means allowing your dog to do whatever he wants to?

Training the dog is like parenting. You should set limits and boundaries, and enforce them consistently.

This consistency would make it quite easier for the dog to master what you want. It would also reduce anxiety in the dog's life, as he knows what to do.

Conclusion

Training a dog requires time, patience and consistency. It can actually be both a simple and enjoyable process if you know how to properly train your dog in obedience. We hope this short guide provided you with useful information and helped you figure out the approach you should take with your own furry friend.

We will be more than happy to learn how this book has helped you in yours and your dog's life and the progress that you have made.

If you feel you have learned something or you think it offered you some value, please take a moment to leave an honest review on Amazon. It would help many future readers who will be forever grateful to you. As we will!

With Best Regards,
Vivaco Books

DISCLAIMER AND/OR LEGAL NOTICES: Every effort has been made to accurately represent this book and it's potential. Results vary with every individual, and your results may or may not be different from those depicted. No promises, guarantees or warranties, whether stated or implied, have been made that you will produce any specific result from this book. Your efforts are individual and unique, and may vary from those shown. Your success depends on your efforts, background and motivation.

The material in this publication is provided for educational and informational purposes. Use of the programs, advice, and information contained in this book is at the sole choice and risk of the reader.

www.ingramcontent.com/pod-product-compliance
Lightning Source LLC
Chambersburg PA
CBHW061058050726

47592CB00004B/1736